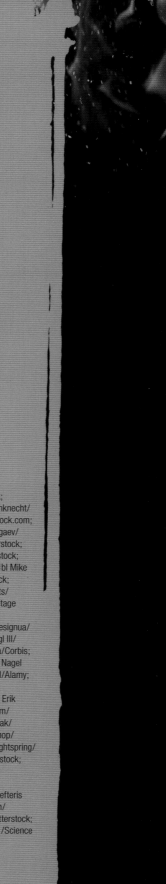

This edition published by Scholastic Inc., 557 Broadway, New York, NY 10012 by arrangement with Egmont UK. Scholastic and associated logos are trademarks and/or registered trademarks of Scholastic Inc.

Scholastic Canada Ltd., Markham, Ontario
Scholastic UK, Coventry, Warwickshire

First published in Great Britain 2015 by Red Shed,
an imprint of Egmont UK Limited
The Yellow Building, 1 Nicholas Road,
London W11 4AN

www.egmont.co.uk

Text copyright © Egmont UK Limited 2015

ISBN 978-0-545-83174-1

Consultancy by Dr Patricia Macnair and Ryan Marek.

A CIP catalogue record for this book is available from the British Library.

The publisher would like to thank the following for permission to reproduce their material. Every care has been taken to trace copyright holders. However, if there have been unintentional omissions or failure to trace copyright holders, we apologize and will, if informed, endeavour to make corrections in any future edition.

(OFC = Outside Front Cover, b = bottom, c = centre, l = left, r = right, t = top)

OFC (volcano spray) KalypsoWorldPhotography/Shutterstock; OFC (volcano cloud) RZ Design/Shutterstock; 2t Olga Nikonova/Shutterstock; 4br Talvi/Shutterstock; 4tr, 13c solarseven/Shutterstock; 5bc Jana Schoenknecht/Shutterstock; 5br Maks Narodenko/Shutterstock; 6bl EpicStockMedia/Shutterstock; 6tr Viahuta/Shutterstock.com; 7bl Hellen Sergeyeva/Shutterstock; 7br G. Light/Shutterstock; 7cr FotografFFF/Shutterstock; 7tr Roman Sigaev/Shutterstock; 8br Peshkova/Shutterstock; 8cl, 8cr, 8cl, 9cr Ostill/Shutterstock; 9br Image Point Fr/Shutterstock; 9tr Andrey Burmakin/Shutterstock; 10bl Peter Waters/Shutterstock; 10br Takahashi Photography/Shutterstock; 10c Lara Zanarini/Shutterstock; 10cl Michael Sheehan/Shutterstock; 10tr Maxene Huiyu/Shu tterstock; 11bl Mike Buckley; 10–11c Lara Zanarini/Shutterstock; 11br Piotr Gatlik/Shutterstock; 11cr Mark Herreid/Shutterstock; 11tl Michael & Patricia Fogden/Getty Images; 11tr Wayne Lawler/Science Photo Library; 12bc Wil Meinderts/Buiten-beeld/Minden Pictures/Getty Images; 12br Dea Picture Library/De Agostini/Getty Images; 12tr Heritage Image Partnership Ltd/Alamy; 12–13 photobess58/Shutterstock; 13bl Sonia Halliday Photographs/Alamy; 13cr Paulo M. F. Pires/Shutterstock; 13tr My Good Images/Shutterstock; 14bc Mopic/Shutterstock; 14c Designua/Shutterstock; 14–15c (volcano) Pablo Hidalgo – Fotos 593/Shutterstock; 14–15c (eruption) John David Bigl III/Shutterstock; 15cr OAR/NATIONAL UNDERSEA RESEARCH PROGRAM (NURP); NOAA; 15tl Alberto Garcia/Corbis; 15tr Dmussman/Shutterstock; 16–17c Mint Images Limited/Alamy; 16bl Loskutnikov/Shutterstock; 16–17 Nagel Photography/Shutterstock; 17cr (squirrel) Vladislav T. Jirousek/Shutterstock; 17br Juniors Bildarchiv GmbH/Alamy; 17cr (beetle) Vblinov/Shutterstock; 17tr All Canada Photos/Alamy; 17tl, 19tl Vadimmmus/Shutterstock; 18bl blickwinkel/Alamy; 18–19c, 19cl Dr. Morley Read/Shutterstock; 19br Bluegreen Pictures/Alamy; 19cr Erik Zandboer/Shutterstock; 20tr Triff/Shutterstock; 20tl silver tiger/Shutterstock; 20 (sunset) MO_SESPremium/Shutterstock; 20 (ground) Sunny Forest/Shutterstock; 20 (tree) Ni Haosheng/Shutterstock; 21l Piotr Krzeslak/Shutterstock; 21bl AFP/Getty Images; 21br Jim Reed/Science Photo Library; 21cr Reed Timmer & Jim Bishop/Science Photo Library; 22b Hung Chung Chih/Shutterstock.com; 22c Benoit Daoust/Shutterstock; 22bc Lightspring/Shutterstock; 23bl US Air Force – digital version c Science Faction/Corbis; 23bc Aleksey Stemmer/Shutterstock; 23c Bayanova Svetlana/Shutterstock; 23cr Levent Konuk/Shutterstock; 23tl FloridaStock/Shutterstock; 24–25c solarseven/Shutterstock; 24bl Stocktrek Images, Inc./Alamy; 24tl NASA/JPL – Caltech/ZMASS; 25br NASA/ESA, J. Hester, A Loll (ASU); 25tr Tristan3D/Shutterstock; 26b Melkor3D/Shutterstock; 26cl Lefteris Papaulakis/Shutterstock.com; 26tr Catmando/Shutterstock; 27br Fotokostic/Shutterstock; 27cl 123Nelson/Shutterstock; 27cr (head) Pindyurin Vasily/Shutterstock; 27cr (body) LilKar/Shutterstock; 27tl Pakmor/Shutterstock; 28r highviews/Shutterstock; 28l Luiz Antonio da Silva/Shutterstock; 29bl Scientifica/Visuals Unlimited, Inc./Science Photo Library; 29br Igor Zh/Shutterstock; 29cl Arena Photo UK/Shutterstock; 29cr scyther5/Shutterstock; 29tl Jiang Hongyan/Shutterstock; 29tr The Oxfordshire Chilli Garden/Alamy; 32 fluke samed/Shutterstock. All textures and illustrated elements are courtesy of Shutterstock.

The Hot Book

Dr. Mike Goldsmith
Miranda Smith

■ SCHOLASTIC
www.scholastic.com

Contents

5   Hot, hot, hot!

6   The science of heat

8   People and heat

10   Animals in the heat

12   Fire

14   Fiery Earth

16   Desert heat

18   Tropical rainforests

20   Hot weather

22   Global warming

24   Hot space

26   Legends of fire and heat

28   Strange but true

30   Glossary

31   Index

Hot, hot, hot!

Without heat, we would not survive for long. The amount of heat inside the bodies of all living things affects the efficiency with which they work. Heat is needed to grow and prepare food; heat affects the planet's weather; and heat plays a vital role in making things that we use every day.

Heat is measured by temperature. Objects that have a high temperature are described as hot. We cannot see heat, but we can both feel and see its effects: watching air shimmering above a hot road; feeling the heat coming from a candle flame; seeing grass turning brown during a hot, dry summer. Our planet runs on heat that comes from deep inside its molten core as well as from our star, the Sun. Throughout the universe, heat is constantly being generated, changed, and used. Heat is everywhere – and sometimes in surprising places!

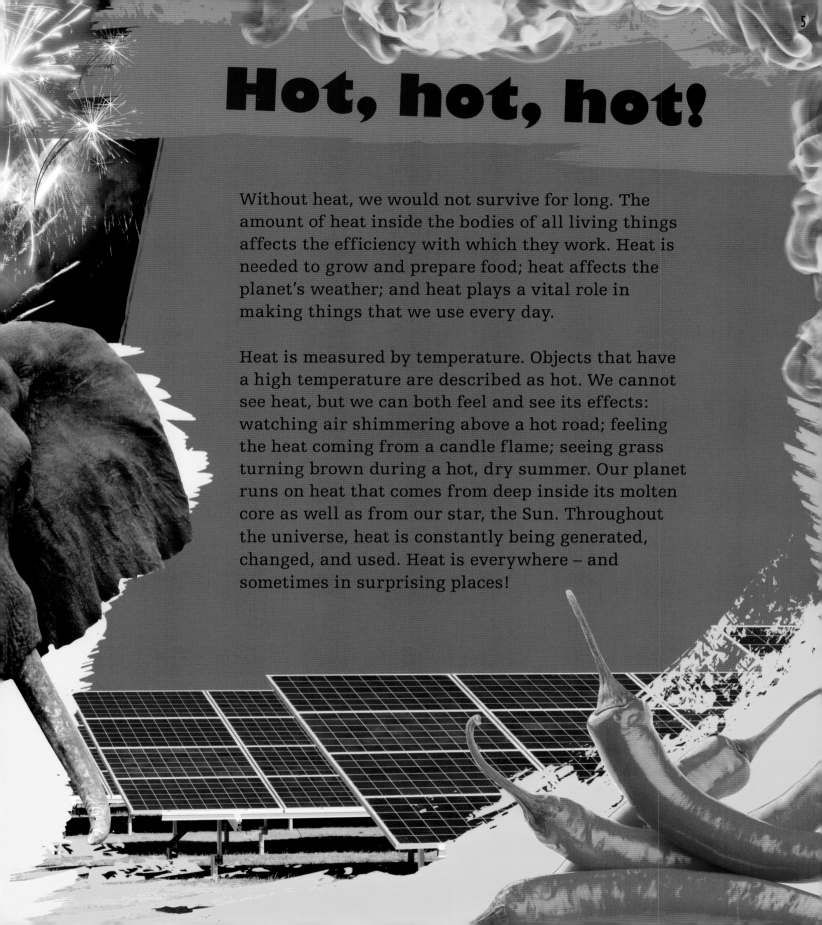

The *science* of **heat**

Heat is a kind of energy that is present in all matter, and heat energy constantly flows into and out of all objects, moving energy from a higher temperature to a lower temperature. Heat energy can be harnessed to do useful and efficient work – factories use it to make everyday materials, and engines burn fuels to power machines.

ENERGY

There are many different kinds of energy, and they can change from one kind to another. For example, the food you eat contains chemical energy that is partly changed into heat energy during digestion to keep your body warm. The hotter something is, the faster the molecules inside it move as its heat energy increases. Without energy, everything comes to a halt.

To stop a car, the brakes must turn the car's kinetic energy into heat energy. This is done when the brake pads clamp down on the brake discs and use friction to generate heat.

FRICTION

Friction happens when any two objects rub against or slide past one another. Friction always slows down a moving object, so when two objects lose speed in this way, they have to release energy; they do this in the form of heat energy. You can feel this when you rub your cold hands together and they get warmer.

Surfers benefit from the friction between the bottom of a wave and the seafloor. The lower part of the wave heats up and slows down, while the upper part continues to travel at high speed, rising up and curling before breaking on the shore. The froth at the top of the wave also provides friction that heats the wave.

HOW HEAT TRAVELS

Heat always moves from a hot object to a cold one until the temperatures equalize. How quickly this can happen depends on the difference in temperature between the two objects and how easily the heat can move.

Convection is the transfer of heat through the movement of a liquid such as water, or a gas such as air. The water in this pot is being heated by the flames while transferring heat upward toward the surface and then up into the air.

Radiation is the transfer of heat by electromagnetic (light and heat) waves through the air. This gas flame is radiating heat upward and outward, to warm the pan and the air around it.

Conduction is the transfer of heat from one molecule to another in a substance. The heat travels from the gas flame and through the glass container into the water.

DID YOU KNOW?

Your computer would be slow and overheat without its heat sink. It cools down the computer by conducting heat away from the central processing unit (CPU) into fins that have a large surface area and can spread the hot air through the rest of the computer. A fan blows out excess hot air.

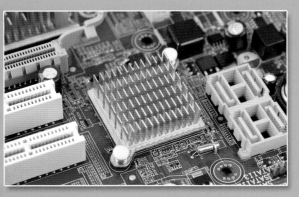

The microprocessor on this computer circuit board is cooled by the heat sink (center) that sits on top of it. Heat sinks are usually made from a metal that's a good conductor of heat.

GETTING BIGGER

Most solids, liquids, and gases expand when they are heated because when their molecules move faster, they bump into each other and move farther apart. Steam engines, rockets, and car engines are all powered by the expansion of gases.

Expanded gas blasts out of the rocket and provides a thrust to propel it in the other direction.

People and heat

Your body makes heat all the time – when your heart beats, when your muscles move, when you digest food, and even when you think! It is very good at keeping its average internal temperature at a steady 98.6°F (37°C). The human body has also evolved ways of coping in hot weather or when attacked by a virus. But it is less prepared to cope with the scorching effects of the Sun.

BLOOD AND SWEAT

When you exercise, blood collects heat as it passes through your muscles. The blood carries this heat to the skin, traveling through a network of blood vessels to just under the skin's surface. When your body is in danger of overheating, these vessels widen to allow more blood to reach the surface, and lose heat to the air more quickly.

Most of the time, the air around you carries heat away from your skin. However, if this does not cool you down enough, you start to sweat. The sweat evaporates from the hot skin, cooling it down.

HEATING UP

When you are too cold, the blood vessels in the skin contract, or narrow, so that blood flow to the skin is reduced and your body retains heat. You may start shivering, which is an involuntary, rapid contraction of the muscles. This extra muscle activity generates more heat and warms you up.

RUNNING A TEMPERATURE

Viruses and bacteria work best at our core temperature of 98.6°F (37°C), so when attacked, your body fights back by raising your temperature. This stops a virus from multiplying and causes it to die. So running a temperature – as long as it does not go too high – can be a good sign!

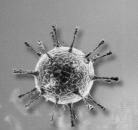

A small amount of sunlight does us good – for example, it helps us to make vitamin D. But it does not take much more to damage us. Our skin contains cells called melanocytes, whose job it is to produce melanin. Melanin traps sunlight so that it does not reach the deep layers of the skin and cause damage there. The more melanin a person's skin contains, the darker brown they appear.

The toughest marathon on Earth is the Badwater Ultramarathon through Death Valley in California, where the temperature reaches 130°F (55°C). Athletes prepare by sweating it out in saunas.

The **average person** has **2.6 million sweat glands** in **their skin**.

BURNING HOT

Our skin is equipped with very sensitive heat-detecting nerve endings, which means we know almost instantly if we are touching something hot. We also have a built-in reaction called a reflex that is very quick – for instance, you automatically pull your hand away from a hot flame before you even think about it. Sometimes the heat is so great that damage is done before you can pull away, and you get burned.

WHEN HEAT WINS

If your body cannot keep cool enough, the result is heat exhaustion. Sufferers become weak and dizzy, with pounding hearts, low blood pressure, and hot, dry skin. It is vital to cool down and drink plenty of fluids.

Cold   Hot

Animals
in the heat

Living in very hot conditions is a challenge for many animals. Most limit their activity to cooler times of the day. Some burrow, or hide in the shade of rocks and vegetation. Many sweat because drying sweat cools the skin. But some animals have even more ingenious ways of beating the heat.

LICKING
Kangaroos lick their arms until they are covered in saliva. When a breeze blows across their wet arms, the saliva evaporates. This carries away body heat and cools the animal.

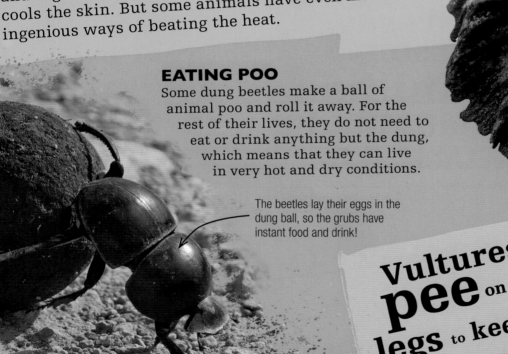

EATING POO
Some dung beetles make a ball of animal poo and roll it away. For the rest of their lives, they do not need to eat or drink anything but the dung, which means that they can live in very hot and dry conditions.

The beetles lay their eggs in the dung ball, so the grubs have instant food and drink!

Vultures **pee** on their legs to keep cool!

When a hive gets too warm, a special bee team keeps cool air flowing by flapping their wings in the same direction.

Costa's hummingbirds travel to stay cool. During winter, they breed in the desert areas of northern Mexico. As the hot summer months begin, they set off for the cooler coastal areas farther north, sometimes as far away as Alaska.

The shovel-snouted lizard runs over hot desert sand very quickly. This short contact with the hot surface means it avoids getting toasted feet!

WATER STORAGE

In Australian summers, the water-holding frog drinks until it is bloated, then covers itself in slime and buries itself in the desert sand. It can stay underground like this for up to two years.

PANTING

Dogs and cats don't sweat, except for the undersides of their paws. Dogs lose heat by panting or staying in the shade. Cats flatten themselves out on a cool surface. Some cats have thick coats to shade them from the sun.

African elephants are the largest land mammals on Earth.

FIERY FACT

The deep-sea Pompeii worm is the most heat-tolerant animal on Earth. It lives near hydrothermal vents in water temperatures of up to 175°F (80°C).

RADIATING

The huge ears of an elephant provide the extra skin needed to radiate away heat. The smaller an animal is, the more skin it has for its volume. So a mouse can get rid of excess heat much more easily than an elephant.

warm air out

cool air in

cool air in

AIR-CONDITIONED

In a termite nest, air shafts at the base of the mound allow cooling air to flow in. Warm air rises up and out through shafts at the top. This maintains a constant temperature of 86°F (30°C) for the gardens of fungi that the termites farm for food.

Fire-breather Antonio Restivo **blew a flame 26.4 feet (8m) high** on January 11, 2011.

Fire

Of all the things that people have discovered, fire is one of the most important. No one knows when this happened, but ash has been found in Wonderwerk Cave, South Africa, suggesting that people there used fire to cook more than a million years ago. Through the ages, people have discovered many different uses for fire.

30,000 ya
CAVE PAINTINGS
Ancient peoples decorated walls of caves with paint made from the charcoal of heated wood. This was mixed with spit or animal fat.

800 BCE
IRON AGE
People learned how to extract iron from rocks by smelting. They used bellows to blow fresh air onto flames and reach a higher temperature.

475 mya
FIRST FIRE
There were no fires on Earth until about 475 mya (million years ago) because there were so few plants on the planet. Plants produce a gas called oxygen, without which no fire can burn.

Early fires would have started with lightning striking dry vegetation from trees very similar to this gingko.

Iron Age spears

FIERY FACT

Firefighters wear clothing made with Kevlar to protect themselves against the intense heat from a fire. Kevlar was invented in 1965 by US chemist Stephanie Kwolek.

WHAT IS FIRE?

Fire is the result of a chemical reaction called combustion, the scientific name for burning. When a fuel such as coal or wood burns, parts of it combine with oxygen in the air. This produces new gases, releasing heat and light as flames.

6CE
FIRE BRIGADE

The first fire brigade was established in Rome. It consisted of 7,000 firefighters called *vigils*.

1110
FIREWORKS

A grand fireworks display was put on for Emperor Huizong of Song in China in 1110. The first fireworks were bamboo shoots filled with gunpowder.

2009
WILDFIRES

The Black Saturday bushfires blazed across Victoria, Australia, in February 2009. Millions of animals and 173 people were killed, and more than one million acres of land were destroyed.

672CE
GREEK FIRE

This weapon is said to have been invented by Callinicus of Heliopolis. A stream of burning liquid – probably containing sulphur or quicklime – was capable of destroying an enemy fleet.

1826
FIRST MATCH

English chemist John Walker discovered by accident that a stick coated with chemicals would burst into flames when scraped across the hearth. He had invented the match!

Fiery Earth

If you were able to drill down 4,000 miles (6,436km) to the center of the Earth, you would find temperatures of around 12,100°F (6,700°C). This internal heat provides energy for our dynamic planet. It pushes parts of Earth's crust around, moving continents, building mountains, and causing volcanoes to erupt.

MOVING CONTINENTS

Earth's surface is broken up into tectonic plates. These float on top of magma (molten rock) and move against one another because of heat currents in the mantle. When the plates meet, they may crash together, pull apart, or scrape past each other. This activity often causes strong earthquakes or volcanoes.

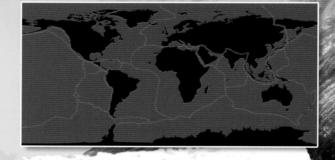

Earth's solid crust is broken up into about eight major tectonic plates and many minor ones. Volcanoes are most likely to occur along the boundaries between the plates.

HEAT STORAGE

Most heat inside Earth is stored in the mantle. Some heat remains from when the planet began to form over 4.6 billion years ago. There is heat from friction caused by denser material sinking and pushing less dense material outward. But up to 90 percent is produced by elements such as uranium, potassium, and thorium decaying and radiating heat as they offload excess energy.

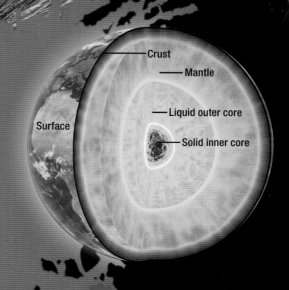

Crust

Mantle

Liquid outer core

Surface

Solid inner core

There are about **1,500** active volcanoes **worldwide.**

Mount Pinatubo erupted in 1991 after lying dormant for 500 years.

HOT SPRINGS

There are many hot springs all over the world. Most are formed from surface water that has seeped underground, heated there, and returned to the surface. In some cases, the water is heated by very hot volcanic rock that is quite close to the surface.

In sub-zero temperatures, Japanese macaques soak in the warmth of a volcanic hot spring.

DID YOU KNOW?

Scientists study volcanoes to further our understanding of the deep Earth and also to warn people if there is likely to be an eruption. They measure the movement or shaking underground – seismicity – as well as changes in gases or the shape of a volcano. The strengths are measured on the Volcanic Explosivity Index (VEI) on a scale of 0 (the smallest) to 8 (the largest).

The water is full of mineral particles such as sulphur, copper, and zinc.

EARTH'S MOST POWERFUL VOLCANOES

Yellowstone, USA
640,000 years ago VEI 8

Mount Tambora, Sumbawa, Indonesia
1815 VEI 7

Krakatoa, Indonesia
1883 VEI 6

Mount Pinatubo, Luzon, Philippines
1991 VEI 6

Mount St Helens, USA
1980 VEI 5

Lascar, Chile
1993 VEI 4

RAINING FIRE

At this very moment, between 15 and 20 volcanoes are erupting around the world, as magma forces its way up from a chamber deep underground. Of the 1,500 active volcanoes worldwide, the biggest are the stratovolcanoes. When these erupt, they blast ash and gas high into the atmosphere, where they travel across the globe.

BLACK SMOKERS

Deep in the ocean, there are areas of the sea floor where water heated by volcanic activity gushes out in black clouds. The water temperature can reach over 750°F (400°C). These hydrothermal vents are home to unique plants and animals that have evolved to flourish in the warmth

Desert heat

A desert is an area where there is less than 10 inches (25cm) of rainfall in a year, but some deserts actually get less than one inch (2.5cm)! Despite this lack of water, deserts are remarkably rich in plant and animal life that has adapted to live in harsh conditions (see also pages 10–11).

HOT DESERTS

Deserts cover almost a third of our planet's surface and are found on every continent. Most of them are hot deserts that are on either side of the Equator around the Tropic of Cancer and the Tropic of Capricorn. What little water these hot deserts receive is lost almost immediately through evaporation.

LIVING IN THE DESERT

Most desert-dwellers live in small villages, some of which are next to fertile oases, so they can grow crops. Many people have to walk long distances each day to the nearest well to fetch water. Other desert peoples live a nomadic life, traveling with their herds and goods to springs or wells.

WATER ILLUSION

In the desert, people are often misled by reflections of the sky off thin layers of hot air near the heated ground. They think they can see an area of water in the distance. This optical illusion is called a mirage.

SINGING DUNES

In the Sahara, the desert wind pushes sand up toward the top of large, crescent-shaped dunes called barchans. When the angle reaches a tipping point of 35°, rivers of sand slide downwards, filling the air with a deep humming sound, like the engine of a plane, that can be heard from up to six miles (9.7km) away. Different dunes sing different notes.

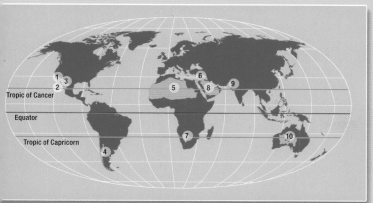

Top 10 Hottest Deserts:

1 Mojave
2 Sonoran
3 Chihuahuan
4 Monte
5 Sahara
6 Syrian
7 Kalahari
8 Arabian
9 Thar
10 Australian

Tropic of Cancer
Equator
Tropic of Capricorn

Women expertly balance clay vessels full of water on their heads in the Thar desert of India and Pakistan. The women collect water daily from a well and carry it back 6 miles (9.7km) in the scorching heat to their villages.

1.6%
of the **world's** population lives in **hot deserts.**

The sand moves downhill at 130ft/s (40m/s), with sand grains colliding about 100 times a second. This turns the face of the dune into a huge loudspeaker.

DID YOU KNOW?

Animals and plants have evolved some intriguing techniques for survival in hot deserts.

Many, like this kangaroo rat, are nocturnal, only emerging from cool underground burrows at night to hunt for food.

The darkling beetle collects moisture on its body from early morning fogs and drinks it as it trickles down.

The Cape ground squirrel has a flattened tail nearly as long as its body, and uses it as shelter during the heat of the day.

The honey mesquite of the Sonoran desert has a tap root up to 190 feet (58m) long to draw water up from deep in the ground.

Tropical rainforests

Tropical rainforests are some of the warmest places on Earth. In their hot and humid climates, it rains nearly every day, and the temperatures fluctuate only a few degrees throughout the year. These forests are perfect habitats for more than half of the world's plant and animal species because there are no food shortages.

HOT RAINFORESTS

Less than seven percent of Earth's surface is covered in tropical rainforests. These are all close to the Equator, where temperatures are high all year round, and the average monthly temperature is more than 75°F (24°C).

Plants in the **Amazon** rainforest produce more than **20%** of the world's **oxygen**.

DAILY WEATHER

Tropical rainforests produce their own weather cycles. In the morning, the sun shines and heats up the forest, causing hot, wet air to rise through the trees and condense to form cumulus clouds above the canopy. In the afternoon, the clouds release rain that filters back down to the forest floor, and the whole cycle begins again.

WARMED BY THE SUN

The trees are always green because there are no seasons, so they grow all the time. The sunlight absorbed by their leaves is converted into chemical energy through the process of photosynthesis. The plants store huge amounts of carbon, releasing oxygen into the atmosphere.

This cross-section of a leaf shows the round, green chloroplasts that absorb sunlight during photosynthesis.

Tropic of Cancer

Equator

Tropic of Capricorn

1 Central America rainforest
2 Amazon rainforest
3 Congo river basin rainforest
4 Madagascar rainforest
5 Southeast Asia rainforest

FALLING FOXES

Increased global warming (see pages 22–23) is threatening many rainforest species. On January 12, 2002, in Australia, temperatures soared to 110°F (43°C) – eight degrees higher than usual. Flying foxes, which doze in the treetops during the day, began to pant and lick their wrists in an attempt to cool themselves. Then they fell dead from the trees.

In total, between 2003 and 2006, heatwaves killed more than 20,000 flying foxes.

LIVING ON AIR

Many plants have adaptations that allow them to flourish in the heat. Epiphytes have adapted to grow in the upper canopy to get as much sunlight as possible. They live on the branches of trees, taking their moisture and nutrients from the air.

DRIP TIP

Thick, leathery, and shiny leaves protect trees against both sunlight and rainfall. Many plants have leaves that are grooved or have long, thin drip spouts that help water slip off, keeping the leaves dry and stopping mold and mildew from forming.

Hot weather

A layer of mixed gases about 500 miles (805km) deep – the atmosphere – surrounds Earth and stops it from becoming too hot or too cold for life. All weather happens in the troposphere, the layer of the atmosphere nearest the planet's surface. Heat energy from the Sun is spread around our planet in the troposphere via winds, clouds, and rain.

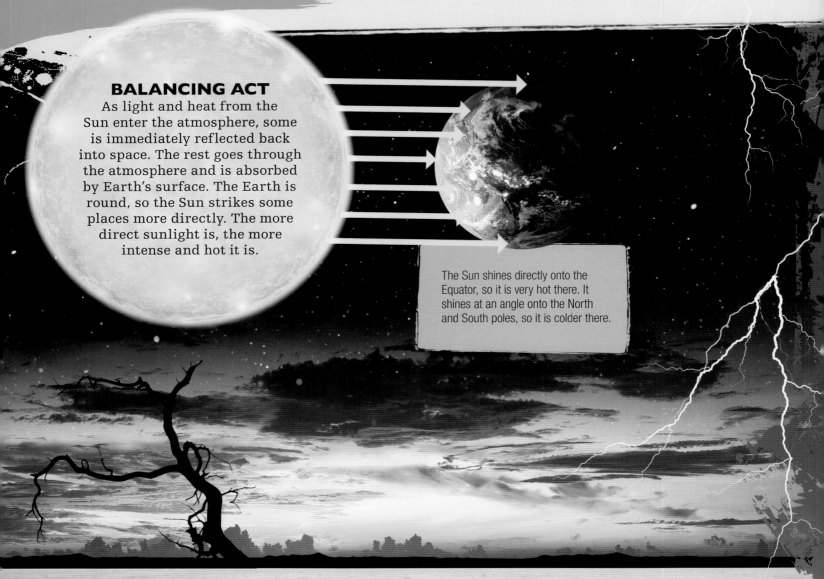

BALANCING ACT
As light and heat from the Sun enter the atmosphere, some is immediately reflected back into space. The rest goes through the atmosphere and is absorbed by Earth's surface. The Earth is round, so the Sun strikes some places more directly. The more direct sunlight is, the more intense and hot it is.

The Sun shines directly onto the Equator, so it is very hot there. It shines at an angle onto the North and South poles, so it is colder there.

EXTREME HEAT
Long periods of heat can cause disasters. Animals and plants die and people are driven out of their homes. And it takes only a spark to start a wildfire in a drought area. Winds can cause the rapid spread of such fires by carrying burning embers to new areas.

Yuma, Arizona has an average of 4,055 hours of sunshine in a year!

HOT LIGHTNING

Lightning is an electric current and not hot in itself. But it travels at more than 136,700mph (220,000kph), causing the air it passes through to heat to an extraordinary 50,430°F (28,000°C) – five times hotter than the surface of the Sun! The air is heated so quickly that the molecules expand and explode, creating the loud noise we call thunder.

SPINNING WINDS

Hot weather fills the atmosphere with energy, sometimes leading to a tornado, in which warm air mixes with cold air and spins around at high speeds. It drags up dust to form a funnel-like shape, which then drifts across the land at up to 70mph (113kph), destroying everything in its path.

There are about **1,800** thunderstorms around the globe **every** day.

DEADLY SANDSTORM

In some parts of the world, there are winds so fierce that they have their own names. One such wind is the simoon, which means "poisonous wind." It affects the deserts of north Africa and Arabia as well as nearby countries. It is very hot, dry, and dusty.

Sandstorms happen when strong winds move over deserts, sucking up sand as they go. Sometimes sand is carried right across continents.

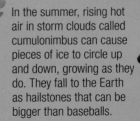

In the summer, rising hot air in storm clouds called cumulonimbus can cause pieces of ice to circle up and down, growing as they do. They fall to the Earth as hailstones that can be bigger than baseballs.

Global warming

Earth is getting warmer, but how do we know this and are we to blame? Scientists are measuring everything from carbon dioxide levels in the air to how many acres of the rainforest are burned down each year, as well as how high sea levels have risen in parts of the world, to establish what damage is being caused.

GREENHOUSE GASES

Greenhouse gases, such as water vapor, carbon dioxide, methane, and ozone in the atmosphere, keep Earth at the right temperature for life by trapping some of the Sun's heat. But the concentration of these gases is increasing, because of our actions, including the burning of fossil fuels and deforestation.

4% reflected by Earth's surface

6% scattered by the atmosphere

19% absorbed by the atmosphere

20% scattered and reflected by clouds

51% absorbed by Earth

CARBON OVERLOAD

We burn fossil fuels to create energy to heat our houses, fuel our cars, grow our food, and make things we use every day. Every time we burn these fuels, carbon dioxide is released into the atmosphere.

Instead of planting more forests, many people are cutting them down for timber or farmland.

DEFORESTATION

Not only are we burning too many fossil fuels, but we are destroying too many rainforests around the world. The balance between carbon dioxide production and absorption cannot be maintained (see pages 18–19), so the Earth is in danger of becoming too warm.

The pollution of the atmosphere by car exhausts causes many premature deaths.

EFFECTS

SOLUTIONS

Melting ice caps are changing life for polar bears. Without as much sea ice, swimming conditions are dangerous and there are fewer seals for them to hunt.

RENEWABLE ENERGY

It is important to find alternative energy sources to fossil fuels. Heat from the Sun can be harnessed to power homes. And the same heat causes the wind to blow for wind power, helps plants to grow for biomass energy, and causes evaporation and rainfall to make hydropower possible.

Wind turbines capture energy from the wind and use it to generate electricity that can be stored until needed.

OUR WORLD IN DANGER

The polar ice caps and glaciers are melting worldwide, causing sea levels to rise. This significantly affects people who live near the coast, as well as wildlife habitats. Warmer air may result in stormier weather and bigger hurricanes. Hotter air means more water evaporation and more rain, which could mean more flooding.

RECYCLING

When you recycle, you are reducing your carbon footprint – the amount of carbon that is emitted when something is made, transported, and used. And it takes 95 percent less energy to recycle a can than it does to make it from raw materials.

If you recycle one aluminum can, it saves enough energy to run a television for three hours!

BIOMASS ENERGY

Plants take carbon out of the atmosphere when they are growing and return it when they are burned. We need to replant forests that we have lost, and choose high-yield crops to use as alternative fuels.

In 2005, storm surges caused by Hurricane Katrina resulted in the devastating flooding of the city of New Orleans.

We can grow plants such as sunflowers and soybeans to produce oil that can be used to make fuels.

Hot space

Look up at the night sky and you will see thousands of stars. In the heart of a living star, hydrogen atoms smash together at a high speed to make heat and light. In the process, they create new helium atoms. When a star dies, many of those atoms are released into space and seed new stars.

DID YOU KNOW?

In space, the hottest stars shine blue-white. The color depends on a star's surface temperature and the amount of energy it emits. Our Sun is a yellow star.

Star surface temperature

54,000°F (~30,000°C)
18,000°F (~10,000°C)
9,900°F (~5,500°C)
7,200°F (~4,000°C)
5,400°F (~3,000°C)

NEBULA

Some nebulae are where stars are made, a kind of stellar nursery. A nebula is an enormous cloud of dust and hydrogen gas. New stars form inside– a part of the cloud contracts and becomes more dense, getting hotter, and eventually fusing the hydrogen to form a new star.

The Pacman Nebula is an area of active star formation 9,200 light years from Earth in the constellation Cassiopeia.

THE SUN

The Sun, our star, generates power – enough to melt a bridge of ice 2 miles (3.2km) wide and 1 mile (1.6km) thick stretching from Earth to the Sun in one second! Deep inside, it is fusing hydrogen atoms together to produce helium. This nuclear fusion gives off light and heat that is driven from the core toward the surface and out into space. This journey can take more than one million years!

The temperature at the Sun's core is an incredible 27 million °F (15 million °C)

SOLAR STORMS

The surface of the Sun is turbulent. Great storms cause giant flares to erupt and stream extra radiation and particles out through space. They can have a serious effect on Earth, interfering with satellites, electrical grids, and communication systems.

HOTTEST PLANET

The second planet from the Sun, Venus, orbits it at a distance of more than 67 million miles (108 million km). The temperature on this planet is hot enough to melt lead – more than 880°F (470°C). This is because Venus has a thick atmosphere made mainly of carbon dioxide. When rays from the Sun reach Venus, their radiation is trapped by this layer, creating a runaway greenhouse effect (see page 22).

TEMPERATURES IN SPACE

The Sun's radiant energy, or rays, travel through space but do not heat it because space is almost empty. It is only when the rays hit matter – Earth, you, or anything made up of atoms – that part of the radiant energy is absorbed and heats up the object.

SUPERNOVA

Although few and far between, stars that are the most massive – eight times the size of the Sun – are able to heat their cores to several billion degrees. When one of these runs out of fuel, it collapses under its own weight and destroys itself in a huge explosion called a supernova.

The stunning Crab Nebula is the remains of a supernova.

Legends of fire and heat

To many people through the ages, fire seemed to have magical properties – it moved and grew, ate fuel, but could be killed by water. Staring into a fire, they could see strange shapes that fed their fearful imaginations. Fiery myths and legends were born in those flickering flames.

In Chinese mythology, the phoenix ate only dewdrops.

FLAME BIRD

It was said that every one thousand years, the phoenix would burn up in the Sun's rays, and from the ashes a new bird would rise. For the ancient Egyptians and Greeks, the phoenix symbolized immortality. In Arabian myths, it sang a song so enchanting that even the Sun god stopped to listen. Today, a person who makes a comeback is said to be "rising like a phoenix."

FIRE FROM A GOD

Ancient Greeks told the story of Prometheus, who gave the secret of fire-making to men and was sentenced to a terrible punishment. He was chained to a rock, and every day an eagle ate his liver. During the night, the liver would grow back, ready for the eagle to start again the next morning.

BREATH OF FIRE

There are legends of dragons all around the world. They are often described as huge, lizard-like monsters that fly, breathe fire, and like to curl up on a mound of treasure. In China, many people believe that they descend from dragons, which they worship as a force for good. Chinese dragons are powerful, strong, and bring good luck to those who deserve it.

Some cultures believe that dragons control water, rain, floods, and hurricanes.

BORN OF FIRE

The salamander is a shy amphibian. But for many, the "fire lizard" was a creature that lived its entire life in fire. In India and Europe during the Middle Ages, a material said to be the solidified breath or hair of the salamander was used to protect precious objects from fire. We now know that the material they used was asbestos, a real fireproof material.

Salamanders were thought to emerge from volcanoes and have the power to control fire.

FIERY FACT

Dancers perform the Chinese dragon dance during Chinese New Year and other festivals. The longer the dragon, the more luck it is thought to bring.

MONSTERS FROM THE EAST

In Arabia, there are many ruins left behind by long-vanished civilizations. In the past, people avoided these places because they thought they contained a race of monsters called efreets. Although not all efreets were bad – some even married humans – many of them were as cruel as they were powerful.

Efreets were said to be giant, winged creatures made from fire.

LAVA CREATURE

Chile is a country rich in volcanoes, and according to local legends, at least one is inhabited by a giant monster called Cherufe. Not only can Cherufe live in molten lava, it is actually made of it. Unfortunately for local villagers, Cherufe is also very happy outside its volcano. What's more, without Cherufe inside to keep it quiet, it is said that the volcano will erupt.

Cherufe enjoys eating people, cooking them as it does so.

Strange but true

Heat is all around you – in your body, in volcanoes, in space . . . it affects every part of your life and everything you do. Here are some of the more extraordinary ways in which heat affects people and other living things on our planet.

FIERY FACT

The hottest man-made temperature ever recorded is 9.9 trillion °F (over 5.5 trillion °C)– 100,000 times hotter than the Sun's interior – when scientists at CERN's Large Hadron Collider collided lead ions in 2012.

The toco toucan has an interesting way of keeping cool. Its enormous beak – about one-third of its length – helps to keep the bird cool. The toucan, like other birds, cannot sweat, so it alters the blood flow to its beak to control the amount of heat that is released or conserved.

The **black circles** around **meerkats' eyes** absorb the **Sun's rays** and **stop them** from **reflecting back** into their **eyes**.

SOLAR POWER

The largest solar kitchen in the world is at the Shirdi Sai Baba temple in India. The 84 rooftop-mounted reflectors help the cooks produce up to 38,500 meals in the middle of the day when the Sun is at its highest in the sky.

CHILIES: HOT OR NOT?

By themselves, they are not! Chilies contain a chemical called capsaicin. This stimulates nerves in your skin and tongue to make your brain think that they are burning. The more chilies you eat, the less the nerves react, and the hotter the chilies you can eat.

The hottest chili in the world is the Smokin Ed's "Carolina Reaper."

On the Spanish island of Lanzarote, off the coast of Morocco, there is a unique restaurant called *El Diablo* (The Devil). The chefs there work in an extraordinary kitchen – they cook food over heat produced by an active volcano! A giant grill has been installed over a cooking pit that has nine layers of volcanic basalt rock as a base. The volcano, which last erupted in 1824, cooks the food at a steady 750°F (400°C).

HOT WORK!

The hottest place of work is probably the Mponeng gold mine in South Africa. It is one of the deepest mines in the world. Just 2.5 miles (4km) below the surface, the temperature of the rock can reach 140°F (60°C). For people to work there, 6,000 tons (5,443 tonnes) of ice a day have to be pumped in, and refrigerated air is blown through the passageways.

BOILING OVER

Compared by area, your body makes more heat than the Sun! The human body creates so much heat that if, after activity, you were able to collect 30 minutes' worth of heat from your entire body, you could boil water!

Roy C. Sullivan, a former park ranger in Shenandoah National Park, Virginia, holds the record for being struck by lightning seven times and surviving!

Glossary

asbestos
A mineral found in the ground. It has fibers and is woven into a cloth that does not burn.

atmosphere
The layer of gases that surrounds a planet or star. Earth's atmosphere is made of air.

atom
A tiny particle of matter, consisting of protons, neutrons, and electrons. Atoms are the smallest particles that can take part in a chemical reaction.

biomass
Plant material used for fuel.

canopy
The layer of the rainforest between the understorey below and emergent layer above. Most rainforest animals live in the canopy.

cell
One of the tiny units that make up all living things.

combustion
The chemical reaction between a fuel and oxygen that produces heat and usually light.

condense
To turn a gas into a liquid. Water is condensed steam.

deforestation
The act of cutting down trees and vegetation to make room for farming or mining, or to use the wood.

digestion
The breaking down of food inside the gut so that it can be used to fuel the body.

electromagnetic
Describes a type of magnet that can be switched on and off. When it is turned on, electricity flows through a coil of wire, creating a magnetic field.

energy
The power to do work. People get energy from food. Engines get energy from fuel such as gasoline.

evaporate
To change from a liquid to a gas.

fossil fuel
A fuel that is formed from the ancient remains of living things. Fossil fuels include coal, oil, and natural gas. They contain high levels of carbon, and they release carbon dioxide when they are burned.

friction
The rubbing of one surface against another surface. Friction slows things down.

greenhouse gas
Any gas in the atmosphere that plays a part in the greenhouse effect – the trapping of heat by gases in a planet's atmosphere. The most important greenhouse gases are carbon dioxide and water vapor.

hydropower
Electricity that is generated using the power of water.

hydrothermal vent
An opening on the seafloor from which very hot, mineral-rich water flows. Also called a black smoker.

ion
An electrically charged atom or group of atoms.

kinetic energy
The amount of work an object can do as a result of its motion. The kinetic energy of a moving object depends on its mass and how fast it is moving.

microprocessor
A computer processor with microscopic electronic circuits and components.

molecule
A chemical unit made up of two or more atoms joined together.

nocturnal
Describes animals that are active during the night.

oases
Places in the desert where underground water comes to the surface and plants can grow. Singular: oasis

photosynthesis
The way in which plants make food. They use the energy in sunlight to turn carbon dioxide and water into sugars. Oxygen is released.

temperature
The measure of how hot or cold something is. Thermometers are used to measure temperature in degrees.

thrust
The force, usually generated by an engine, that pushes a vehicle forward.

troposphere
The layer of air about 8 miles (13km) thick just above the surface of Earth.

turbine
A wheel with curved blades that is spun by the movement of a gas or liquid. Turbines drive machines that make electricity.

virus
The tiniest type of germ. A virus takes over the cells of a living thing to make copies of itself.

ABBREVIATIONS

BCE
Before the Common Era

CE
Common Era

mya
Million years ago

ya
Years ago

Index

A

alternative energy 23
ancient Egyptians 26
ancient Greeks 26
animals 10–11, 13,
  15, 17, 18, 20, 28
asbestos 27
atmosphere, Earth
  15, 18, 20–21, 22–23
atmosphere, Venus
  25

B

bacteria 8
bees 10
biomass energy 23
blood 8–9, 28
braking 6
burning 6, 9, 12–13,
  20, 22–23, 26

C

Callinicus of
  Heliopolis 13
Cape ground squirrel
  17
carbon 18, 22–23
carbon dioxide 22, 25
cars 6–7, 22
cats 11
cave painting 12
chilies 29
combustion 13
computers 7
conduction 7
convection 7
cooking 12, 27, 28, 29

D

darkling beetle 17
Death Valley,
  California 9
deforestation 22
deserts 10–11, 16–17,
  21

digestion 6, 8
dogs 11
dragons 26, 27
dung beetles 10

E

Earth 5, 14–15, 18,
  22–23, 24
electricity 23
electromagnetic
  waves 7
elephants 11
energy 5, 6–7, 14, 18,
  20, 21, 22, 23, 24, 25
engines 6–7
Equator 16–17, 18–19,
  20
evaporation 16, 23
expansion 6, 21

F

factories 6
fire 12–13, 15, 20,
  26–27
fire-breathing 12
fire brigade 13
firefighters 13
fireworks 13
flooding 26, 23
flying foxes 19
food 5, 6, 8, 10–11, 17,
  18, 22, 29
fossil fuels 22–23
friction 6, 14
fuel 6, 13, 23, 25

G

gold mine 29
global warming 19,
  22–23
Greek fire 13
greenhouse gases 22,
  25
gunpowder 13

H

heat exhaustion 9
heat sink 7
heatwaves 19
honey mesquite bush
  17
hot springs 15
human body 6, 8–9,
  29
hummingbirds 10
hurricanes 23, 26
hydropower 23
hydrothermal vents
  11, 15

I

Iron Age 12

K

kangaroo rat 17
kangaroos 10
Kevlar 13
Kwolek, Stephanie 13

M

macaques 15
matches 13
meerkats 28
melanin 9
mirages 16
molecules 6–7, 21
monsters 27
mountains 14
muscles 8

N

nebulae 24
nuclear fusion 24

O

oases 16
oxygen 12, 13, 18

P

panting 11, 19
phoenix 26
photosynthesis 18
plants 12, 15, 17,
  18–19, 20, 23
Prometheus 26

R

radiation 7, 11, 14,
  24–25
rainforests 18–19, 22
recycling 23
reflexes 9
rockets 7

S

salamanders 27
sandstorms 21
shade 10, 11
shivering 8
singing dunes 16–17
skin 8–9, 10–11
smelting 12
solar cooker 28
solar storms 24
space 24–25
stars 24–25
Sullivan, Roy C. 29
summer 5, 10–11, 21
Sun 5, 8, 9, 11, 18–19,
  20–21, 22–23, 24–25,
  26, 28–29
supernova 25
surfing 6
sweat 8–9, 10–11, 28

T

tectonic plates 14
temperature 5, 6–7,
  8–9, 11, 14–15,
  18–19, 22, 24–25,
  28–29
termites 11
thunderstorms 21
toco toucan 28
tornados 21

U

universe 5

V

Venus 25
viruses 8
vitamins 9
volcanoes 14–15, 26,
  29
vultures 10

W

Walker, John 13
water-holding frogs
  11
weather 5, 8, 18,
  20–21, 23
wildfires 13, 20
wind power 23
worms 11